BY ADRIENNE RICH

Dark Fields of the Republic: Poems 1991–1995

What Is Found There: Notebooks on Poetry and Politics

Collected Early Poems 1950–1970

An Atlas of the Difficult World: Poems 1988–1991

Time's Power: Poems 1985–1988

Blood, Bread, and Poetry: Selected Prose 1979–1986

Your Native Land, Your Life

The Fact of a Doorframe: Poems Selected and New 1950–1984

Sources

A Wild Patience Has Taken Me This Far

On Lies, Secrets, and Silence: Selected Prose 1966–1978

The Dream of a Common Language

Twenty-one Love Poems

Of Woman Born: Motherhood as Experience and Institution

Poems: Selected and New, 1950–1974

Diving into the Wreck

The Will to Change

Leaflets

Necessities of Life

Snapshots of a Daughter-in-Law

The Diamond Cutters

A Change of World

MIDNIGHT
SALVAGE

Presented by

George Hansen

PACIFIC
GROVE
PUBLIC
LIBRARY

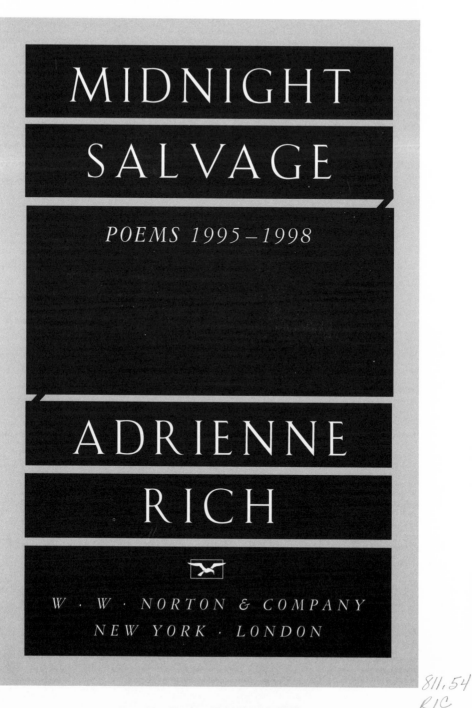

MIDNIGHT SALVAGE

POEMS 1995–1998

ADRIENNE RICH

W · W · NORTON & COMPANY

NEW YORK · LONDON

For information about permission to reproduce selections from this book,
write to Permissions, W. W. Norton & Company, Inc., 500 Fifth Avenue,
New York, NY 10110.

The text of this book is composed in Garamond no. 3 with
the display set in Bauer Text Initials
Desktop composition by Justine Burkat Trubey
Manufacturing by Courier Companies
Book design by Antonina Krass

Library of Congress Cataloging-in-Publication Data

Rich, Adrienne Cecile.
Midnight salvage : poems, 1995–1998 / Adrienne Rich.
p.   cm.
ISBN 0-393-046282-6
I. Title
PS3535.I233M5 1999
811'.54—dc21   98-19293
CIP

W. W. Norton & Company, Inc., 500 Fifth Avenue, New York, NY 10110
http://www.wwnorton.com

W. W. Norton & Company Ltd., 10 Coptic Street, London CW1A 1PU

1 2 3 4 5 6 7 8 9 0

CONTENTS

I don't know how to measure happiness. The issue is happiness, there is no other issue, or no other issue one has a right to think about for other people, to think about politically, but I don't know how to measure happiness.

—George Oppen, letter to June Oppen Degnan, August 5, 1970

THE ART OF TRANSLATION

1

To have seen you exactly, once:
red hair over cold cheeks fresh from the freeway
your lingo, your daunting and dauntless
eyes. But then to lift toward home, mile upon mile
back where they'd barely heard your name
—neither as terrorist nor as genius would they detain you—

to wing it back to my country bearing
your war-flecked protocols—

that was a mission, surely: my art's pouch
crammed with your bristling juices
sweet dark drops of your spirit
that streaked the pouch, the shirt I wore
and the bench on which I leaned.

2

It's only a branch like any other
green with the flare of life in it
and if I hold this end, you the other
that means it's broken

broken between us, broken despite us
broken and therefore dying
broken by force, broken by lying
green, with the flare of life in it

3

But say we're crouching on the ground like children
over a mess of marbles, soda caps, foil, old foreign coins
—the first truly precious objects. Rusty hooks, glass.

Say I saw the earring first but you wanted it.
Then you wanted the words I'd found. I'd give you
the earring, crushed lapis if it were,

I would look long at the beach glass and the sharded self
of the lightbulb. Long I'd look into your hand
at the obsolete copper profile, the cat's-eye, the lapis.

Like a thief I would deny the words, deny they ever
existed, were spoken, or could be spoken,
like a thief I'd bury them and remember where.

4

The trade names follow trade
the translators stopped at passport control:
Occupation: no such designation—
Journalist, maybe spy?

That the books are for personal use
only—could I swear it?
That not a word of them
is contraband—how could I prove it?

1995

FOR AN ANNIVERSARY

The wing of the osprey lifted
over the nest on Tomales Bay
into fog and difficult gust
raking treetops from Inverness Ridge on over
The left wing shouldered into protective
gesture the left wing we thought broken

and the young beneath in the windy nest
creaking there in their hunger
and the tides beseeching, besieging
the bay in its ruined languor

1996

MIDNIGHT SALVAGE

1

Up skyward through a glazed rectangle I
sought the light of a so-called heavenly body
: : a planet or our moon in some event and caught

nothing nothing but a late wind
pushing around some Monterey pines
themselves in trouble and rust-limbed

Nine o'clock : : July : the light
undrained : : that blotted blue
that lets has let will let

thought's blood ebb between life- and death-time
darkred behind darkblue
bad news pulsing back and forth of "us" and "them"

And all I wanted was to find an old
friend an old figure an old trigonometry
still true to our story in orbits flaming or cold

2

Under the conditions of my hiring
I could profess or declare anything at all
since in that place nothing would change
So many fountains, such guitars at sunset

Did not want any more to sit under such a window's
deep embrasure, wisteria bulging on spring air
in that borrowed chair
with its collegiate shield at a borrowed desk

under photographs of the spanish steps, Keats' death mask
and the english cemetery all so under control and so eternal
in burnished frames : : or occupy the office
of the marxist-on-sabbatical

with Gramsci's fast-fading eyes
thumbtacked on one wall opposite a fading print
of the same cemetery : : had memories
and death masks of my own : : could not any more

peruse young faces already straining for
the production of slender testaments
to swift reading and current thinking : : would not wait
for the stroke of noon to declare all passions obsolete

Could not play by the rules
in that palmy place : : nor stand at lectern professing
anything at all
                    in their hire

3

Had never expected hope would form itself
completely in my time : : was never so sanguine
as to believe old injuries could transmute easily
through any singular event or idea : : never
so feckless as to ignore the managed contagion
of ignorance the contrived discontinuities
the felling of leaders and future leaders
the pathetic erections of soothsayers

But thought I was conspiring, breathing-along
with history's systole-diastole
twenty thousand leagues under the sea a mammal heartbeat
sheltering another heartbeat
plunging from the Farallons all the way to Baja
sending up here or there a blowhole signal
and sometimes beached
making for warmer waters
where the new would be delivered : : though I would not see it

4

But neither was expecting in my time
to witness this : : wasn't deep
lucid or mindful you might say enough
to look through history's bloodshot eyes
into this commerce this dreadnought wreck cut loose
from all vows, oaths, patents, compacts, promises : :

                                                    To see

not O my Captain
fallen cold & dead by the assassin's hand

but cold alive & cringing : : drinking with the assassins
in suit of noir Hong Kong silk
pushing his daughter in her famine-
waisted flamingo gown
out on the dance floor with the traffickers
in nerve gas saying to them *Go for it*
and to the girl *Get with it*

5

When I ate and drank liberation once I walked
arm-in-arm with someone who said she had something to teach me
It was the avenue and the dwellers
free of home : roofless : : women
without pots to scour or beds to make
or combs to run through hair
or hot water for lifting grease or cans
to open or soap to slip in that way
under arms then beneath breasts then downward to thighs

Oil-drums were alight under the freeway
and bottles reached from pallets of cardboard corrugate
and piles of lost and found to be traded back and forth
and figures arranging themselves from the wind
Through all this she walked me : : And said
My name is Liberation and I come from here
Of what are you so afraid?

We've hung late in the bars like bats
kissed goodnight at the stoplights
—did you think I wore this city without pain?
did you think I had no family?

6

Past the curve where the old craftsman was run down
there's a yard called Midnight Salvage
He was walking in the road which was always safe
The young driver did not know that road
its curves or that people walked there
or that you could speed yet hold the curve
watching for those who walked there
such skills he did not have being in life unpracticed

but I have driven that road in madness and driving rain
thirty years in love and pleasure and grief-blind
on ice I have driven it and in the vague haze of summer
between clumps of daisies and sting of fresh cowflop odors
lucky I am I hit nobody old or young
killed nobody left no trace
practiced in life as I am

7

This horrible patience which is part of the work
This patience which waits for language for meaning for the
                least sign
This encumbered plodding state doggedly dragging
the IV up and down the corridor
with the plastic sack of bloodstained urine

Only so can you start living again
waking to take the temperature of the soul
when the black irises lean at dawn
from the mouth of the bedside pitcher
This condition in which you swear *I will*
submit to whatever poetry is
I accept no limits   Horrible patience

8

You cannot eat an egg   You don't know where it's been
The ordinary body of the hen
vouchsafes no safety   The countryside refuses to supply
Milk is powdered   meat's in both senses high

Old walls the pride of architects   collapsing
find us in crazed niches   sleeping like foxes
we wanters we unwanted we
wanted for the crime of being ourselves

Fame slides on its belly like any other animal after food
Ruins are disruptions of system leaking in
weeds and light   redrawing
the City of Expectations

You cannot eat an egg   Unstupefied not unhappy
we braise wild greens and garlic   feed the feral cats
and when the fog's irregular documents break open
scan its fissures for young stars
                    in the belt of Orion

1996

CHAR

1

There is bracken there is the dark mulberry
there is the village where no villager survived
there are the hitlerians there are the foresters
feeding the partisans from frugal larders

there is the moon ablaze in every quarter
there is the moon "of tin and sage" and unseen pilots dropping
explosive gifts into meadows of fog and crickets
there is the cuckoo and the tiny snake

there is the table set at every meal
for freedom whose chair stays vacant
the young men in their newfound passions
(Love along with them the ones they love)

Obscurity, code, the invisible existence
of a thrush in the reeds, the poet watching
as the blood washes off the revolver in the bucket
Redbreast, your song shakes loose a ruin of memories

A horrible day . . . Perhaps he knew, at that final instant?
The village had to be spared at any price . . .
How can you hear me? I speak from so far . . .
The flowering broom hid us in a blazing yellow mist . . .

2

This war will prolong itself beyond any platonic armistice. The implanting of political concepts will go on amid upheavals and under cover of self-confident hypocrisy. Don't smile. Thrust aside both skepticism and resignation and prepare your soul to face an intramural confrontation with demons as cold-blooded as microbes.

The poet in wartime, the Surréalistes' younger brother
turned realist (*the village had to be spared at any price*)
all eyes on him in the woods crammed with maquisards ex-
pecting him to signal to fire and save their comrade
shook his head and watched Bernard's execution
knowing that *the random shooting of a revolver*
may be *the simplest surreal act* but never
changes the balance of power and that real acts are not simple
The poet, prone to exaggerate, thinks clearly under torture

knowing the end of the war
would mean no end to the microbes frozen in each soul
the young freedom fighters
in love with the Resistance
fed by a thrill for violence
familiar as his own jaw under the razor

3

Insoluble riverrain conscience echo of the future
I keep vigil for you here by the reeds of Elkhorn Slough
and the brown mouth of the Salinas River going green
where the white egret fishes the fragile margins
Hermetic guide in resistance I've found you and lost you
several times in my life   You were never just
the poet appalled and transfixed by war you were the maker
of terrible delicate decisions and that did not smudge
your sense of limits   You saw squirrels crashing
from the tops of burning pines when the canister exploded
and worse and worse and you were in charge of every risk
the incendiary motives of others were in your charge
and the need for a courage wrapped in absolute tact
and you decided and lived like that and you
held poetry at your lips a piece of wild thyme ripped
from a burning meadow a mimosa twig
from still unravaged country   You kept your senses
about you like that and like this I keep vigil for you.

1996

MODOTTI

Your footprints of light on sensitive paper
that typewriter you made famous
my footsteps following you up stair-
wells of scarred oak and shredded newsprint
these windowpanes smeared with stifled breaths
corridors of tile and jaundiced plaster
if this is where I must look for you
then this is where I'll find you

From a streetlamp's wet lozenge bent
on a curb plastered with newsprint
the headlines aiming straight at your eyes
to a room's dark breath-smeared light
these footsteps I'm following you with
down tiles of a red corridor
if this is a way to find you
of course this is how I'll find you

Your negatives pegged to dry in a darkroom
rigged up over a bathtub's lozenge
your footprints of light on sensitive paper
stacked curling under blackened panes
the always upstairs of your hideout
the stern exposure of your brows
—these footsteps I'm following you with
aren't to arrest you

The bristling hairs of your eyeflash
that typewriter you made famous
your enormous will to arrest and frame

what was, what is, still liquid, flowing
your exposure of manifestos, your
lightbulb in a scarred ceiling
well if this is how I find you
Modotti so I find you

In the red wash of your darkroom
from your neighborhood of volcanoes
to the geranium nailed in a can
on the wall of your upstairs hideout
in the rush of breath a window
of revolution allowed you
on this jaundiced stair in this huge lashed eye

                                              these

footsteps I'm following you with

1996

SHATTERED HEAD

A life hauls itself uphill
    through hoar-mist steaming
the sun's tongue licking
    leaf upon leaf into stricken liquid
When? When? cry the soothseekers
    but time is a bloodshot eye
seeing its last of beauty its own
    foreclosure
                a bloodshot mind
finding itself unspeakable
    What is the last thought?
Now I will let you know?
    or, *Now I know?*
(porridge of skull-splinters, brain tissue
    mouth and throat membrane, cranial fluid)

Shattered head on the breast
    of a wooded hill
laid down there endlessly so
    tendrils soaked into matted compost
become a root
    torqued over the faint springhead
groin whence illegible
    matter leaches: worm-borings, spurts of silt
volumes of sporic changes
    hair long blown into far follicles
blasted into a chosen place

Revenge on the head (genitals, breast, untouched)
    revenge on the mouth

packed with its inarticulate confessions
        revenge on the eyes
green-gray and restless
        revenge on the big and searching lips
                                the tender tongue
revenge on the sensual, on the nose the
        carrier of history
revenge on the life devoured
in another incineration

You can walk by such a place, the earth is made of them
where the stretched tissue of a field or woods is humid
        with belovéd matter
the soothseekers have withdrawn
you feel no ghost, only a sporic chorus
when that place utters its worn sigh
        let us have peace

And the shattered head answers back
        *I believed I was loved, I believed I loved,
        who did this to us?*

1996–97

1941

In the heart of pain where mind is broken
and consumed by body, I sit like you
on the rocky shore   (like you, not with you)

A windmill shudders, great blades cleave the air and corn is ground
for a peasant century's bread and fear of hunger
(like that, but not like that)

Pewter sails drive down green water
barges shoulder fallowing fields
(Like then, not then)

If upstairs in the mill sunrise fell low and thin
on the pierced sleep of children hidden in straw
where the mauled hen had thrashed itself away

if some lost their heads and ran
if some were dragged

if some lived and grew old remembering
how the place by itself was not evil
had water, spiders, a cat

if anyone asked me—

How did you get here anyway?
Are you the amateur of drought? the collector
of rains? are you poetry's inadmissible
untimely messenger?

By what right?
In whose name?
Do you

1997

LETTERS TO A YOUNG POET

1

Your photograph won't do you justice
those wetted anthill mounds won't let you focus
that lens on the wetlands

five swans chanting overhead
distract your thirst for closure
and quick escape

2

Let me turn you around in your frozen nightgown and say
one word to you: Ineluctable

—meaning, you won't get quit
of this: the worst of the new news

history running back and forth
panic in the labyrinth

—I will not touch you further:
your choice to freeze or not

to say, you and I are caught in
a laboratory without a science

3

Would it gladden you to think
poetry could purely

take its place beneath lightning sheets
or fogdrip   live its own life

screamed at, howled down
by a torn bowel of dripping names

—composers visit Terezin, film-makers Sarajevo
Cabrini-Green or Edenwald Houses

    ineluctable

if a woman as vivid as any artist
can fling any day herself from the 14th floor

would it relieve you to decide   *Poetry*
doesn't make this happen?

4

From the edges of your own distraction turn
the cloth-weave up, its undersea-fold venous

with sorrow's wash and suck, pull and release,
        annihilating rush

to and fro, fabric of caves, the onset of your fear
kicking away their lush and slippery flora nurseried
        in liquid glass

trying to stand fast in rootsuck, in distraction,
        trying to wade this
undertow of utter repetition

Look: with all my fear I'm here with you, trying what it
        means, to stand fast; what it means to move

5

Beneaped. Rowboat, pirogue, caught between the lowest
and highest tides of spring. Beneaped. Befallen,
becalmed, benighted, yes, begotten.
—*Be*—infernal prefix of the actionless.
—*Be*—as in Sit, Stand, Lie, Obey.
The dog's awful desire that takes his brain
and lays it at the boot-heel.

You can be like this forever—*Be*
as without movement.

6

But this is how
I come, anyway, pushing up from below
my head wrapped in a chequered scarf a lanterned helmet on this
        head
pushing up out of the ore
this sheeted face this lanterned head facing the seep of death
my lips having swum through silt
    clearly pronouncing
Hello and farewell

Who, anyway, wants to know
this pale mouth, this stick
of crimson lipsalve Who my
dragqueen's vocal chords my bitter beat
my overshoulder backglance flung
at the great strophes and antistrophes
my chant my ululation my sacred parings
nails, hair my dysentery my hilarious throat

my penal colony's birdstarved ledge my face downtown
in films by Sappho and Artaud?

Everyone.   For a moment.

7

It's not the déjà vu that kills
it's the foreseeing
the head that speaks from the crater

I wanted to go somewhere
the brain had not yet gone
I wanted not to be
there so alone.

1997

CAMINO REAL

Hot stink of skunk
crushed at the vineyards' edge

hawk-skied, carrion-clean
clouds ranging themselves
over enormous autumn

that scribble   edged and skunky
as the great road winds on
toward my son's house seven hours south

Walls of the underpass
smudged and blistered eyes gazing from armpits
THE WANTER WANTED   ARMED IN LOVE AND
            DANGEROUS
WANTED FOR WANTING

To become the scholar of : :
: : to list compare contrast events to footnote lesser evils
calmly to note "bedsprings"
describe how they were wired
to which parts of the body

to make clear-eyed assessments of the burnt-out eye: : investigate
the mouth-bit and the mouth
the half-swole slippery flesh the enforced throat
the whip they played you with the backroad games the beatings by
        the river
O to list collate commensurate to quantify:
I was the one, I suffered, I was there

never
to trust to memory only

to go back   notebook in hand
dressed as no one there was dressed

over and over to quantify
on a gridded notebook page

The difficulty of proving
such things were done for no reason
that every night
"in those years"
people invented reasons for torture

Asleep now,   head in hands
hands over ears   O you
Who do this work
every one of you
every night

Driving south: santabarbara's barbarous
landscaped mind: lest it be forgotten
in the long sweep downcoast

let it not be exonerated

but O the light
on the raw Pacific silks

Charles Olson: "Can you afford not to make
                        the magical study
                                which happiness is?"

I take him to mean
that happiness is in itself a magical study
a glimpse of the *unhandicapped life*
as it might be for anyone, somewhere

a kind of alchemy, a study of transformation
else it withers, wilts

—that happiness is not to be
mistrusted or wasted
though it ferment in grief

George Oppen to June Degnan: "I don't know how
to measure happiness"
—Why measure? in itself it's the measure—

at the end of a day
            of great happiness if there be such a day

drawn by love's unprovable pull

I write this, sign it
                    Adrienne

1997

PLAZA STREET AND FLATBUSH

1

On a notepad on a table
tagged for the Goodwill
the word   *Brooklyn*

on the frayed luggage label
the matchbox cover
the name   *Brooklyn*

in steel-cut script on a watermarked form
on a postcard postmarked 1961
the word   *Brooklyn*

on the medal for elocution
on the ashtray with the bridge
the inscription   *Brooklyn*

in the beige notebook
of the dead student's pride
in her new language

on the union card   the love letter
the mortgaged insurance policy
somewhere it would say,   *Brooklyn*

on the shear of the gull
on the ramp that sweeps
to the great cable-work

on the map of the five boroughs
the death certificate
the last phone bill

in the painter's sighting
of light unseen
till now, in Brooklyn

2

If you had been required
to make inventory
of everything in the apartment

if you had had to list
the acquisitions of a modest life
punctuated with fevers of shopping

—a kind of excitement for her
but also a bandage
over bewilderment

and for him, the provider
the bandage of providing
for everyone

if you had had to cram the bags
with unworn clothing unused linens
bought by a woman

who but just remembered
being handed through the window
of a train in Russia

if you had had to haul
the bags to the freight elevator
if you had been forced to sign

a declaration of all
possessions kept or given away
in all the old apartments

in one building say
at Plaza and Flatbush
or on Eastern Parkway?

Art doesn't keep accounts
though artists
do as they must

to stay alive
and tend their work
art is a register of light

3

The painter taking her moment
—a rift in the clouds—
and pulling it out

—mucous strand, hairy rootlet
sticky clew to the labyrinth
pulling and pulling

forever or as long
as this grain of this universe
will be tested

the painter seizing the light
of creation
giving it back to its creatures

headed under the earth

1997

SEVEN SKINS

1

Walk along back of the library
in 1952
someone's there to catch your eye
Vic Greenberg in his wheelchair
paraplegic GI–
Bill of Rights Jew
graduate student going in
by the only elevator route
up into the great stacks where
all knowledge should and is
and shall be stored like sacred grain
while the loneliest of lonely
American decades goes aground
on the postwar rock
and some unlikely
shipmates found ourselves
stuck amid so many smiles

Dating Vic Greenberg you date
crutches and a chair
a cool wit an outrageous form:
"—just back from a paraplegics' conference,
guess what the biggest meeting was about—
Sex with a Paraplegic!—for the wives—"
In and out of cabs his chair
opening and closing round his

electrical monologue the air
furiously calm around him
as he transfers to the crutches

But first you go for cocktails
in his room at Harvard
he mixes the usual martinis, plays Billie Holiday
talks about Melville's vision of evil
and the question of the postwar moment:
Is there an American civilization?
In the bathroom huge
grips and suction-cupped
rubber mats long-handled sponges
the reaching tools a veteran's benefits
in plainest sight

And this is only memory, no more
so this is how you remember

Vic Greenberg takes you to the best restaurant
which happens to have no stairs
for talk about movies, professors, food
Vic orders wine and tastes it
you have lobster, he Beef Wellington
the famous dessert is baked alaska
ice cream singed in a flowerpot
from the oven, a live tulip inserted there

Chair to crutches, crutches to cab
chair in the cab and back to Cambridge
memory shooting its handheld frames
Shall I drop you, he says, or shall
we go back to the room for a drink?
It's the usual question
a man has to ask it
a woman has to answer
you don't even think

2

What a girl I was then what a body
ready for breaking open like a lobster
what a little provincial village
what a hermit crab seeking nobler shells
what a beach of rattling stones what an offshore raincloud
what a gone-and-come tidepool

what a look into eternity I took and did not return it
what a book I made myself
what a quicksilver study
bright little bloodstain
liquid pouches escaping

What a girl pelican-skimming over fear what a mica lump
            splitting
into tiny sharp-edged mirrors through which
the sun's eclipse could seem normal
what a sac of eggs what a drifting flask
eager to sink   to be found
to disembody   what a mass of swimmy legs

3

Vic into what shoulder could I have pushed your face
laying hands first on your head
onto whose thighs pulled down your head
which fear of mine would have wound itself
around which of yours   could we have taken it   nakedness
without sperm   in what insurrectionary
convulsion would we have done it   mouth to mouth
mouth-tongue to vulva-tongue to anus   earlobe to nipple
what seven skins each have to molt what seven shifts
what tears boil up through sweat to bathe
what humiliatoriums   what layers of imposture

What heroic tremor
released into pure moisture
might have soaked our shape   two-headed   avid
into your heretic
linen-service
sheets?

1997

"THE NIGHT HAS A THOUSAND EYES"

1

The taxi meter clicking up
loose change who can afford to pay

basalt blurring spectral headlights
darkblue stabbed with platinum

raincoats glassy with evening wet
the city gathering

itself for darkness
into a bitter-chocolate vein

the east side with its trinkets
the west side with its memories

2

Wherever you had to connect:
question of passport, glances, bag

dumped late on the emptied carousel
departure zones

where all could become mislaid, disinvented
undocumented, unverified

all but the footprint of your soul
in the cool neutral air

till the jumbo jet groaned and gathered
itself over Long Island

gathered you into your earth-craving
belly-self, that desire

3

Gaze through the sliced-glass window
nothing is foreign here

nothing you haven't thought or taught
nothing your thumbnail doesn't know

your old poets and painters knew it
knocking back their wine

you're just in a cab driven wild
on the FDR by a Russian Jew

who can't afford to care if he lives or dies
you rode with him long ago

4

Between two silvered glass urns an expensive
textile is shouldered

it's after dark now, floodlight
pours into the wired boutique

there are live roses in the urns
there are security codes

in the wall   there are children, dead, near death
whose fingers worked this

intricate
desirable thing

—nothing you haven't seen on your palm
nothing your thumbnail doesn't know

5

After one stroke she looks at the river
remembers her name—Muriel

writes it in her breath
on the big windowpane

never again perhaps
to walk in the city freely

but here is her landscape this old
industrial building converted

for artists
her river   *the Lordly Hudson*

Paul named it   *which has no peer*
in Europe or the East

her mind on that water   widening

6

Among five men walks a woman
tall as the tallest man, taller than several

a mixed creature
from country poverty   good schooling

and from that position seeing
further than many

beauty, fame, notwithstanding   standing
for something else

—Where do you come from?—
—Como tú, like you, from nothing—

Julia de Burgos, of herself, fallen
in Puerto Rican Harlem

7

Sometime tonight you'll fall down
on a bed far from your heart's desire

in the city as it is
for you now: her face or his

private across an aisle
throttling uptown

bent over clasped hands or
staring off then suddenly glaring:

Back off! Don't ask!   you will meet those eyes
(none of them meeting)

8

The wrapped candies from Cleveland
The acclaim of East St. Louis

deadweight trophies borne
through *interboro fissures of the mind*

in search of Charlie Parker
—Where are you sleeping tonight? with whom?

in crippled Roebling's harbor room
where he watched his bridge transpire?—

Hart   Miles   Muriel   Julia   Paul
you will meet the eyes you were searching for

and the day will break

as we say, it breaks
as we don't say, of the night

as we don't say of the night

1997

RUSTED LEGACY

Imagine a city where nothing's
forgiven   your deed adheres
to you like a scar, a tattoo   but almost everything's
forgotten   deer flattened leaping a highway for food
the precise reason for the shaving of the confused girl's head
the small boys' punishing of the frogs
—a city memory-starved but intent on retributions
Imagine the architecture   the governance
the men and the women in power
—tell me if it is not true you still
          live in that city.

Imagine a city partitioned   divorced from its hills
where temples and telescopes used to probe the stormy codices
a city brailling through fog
thicket and twisted wire
into dark's velvet dialectic
sewers which are also rivers
art's unchartered aquifers   the springhead
sprung open in civic gardens left unlocked at night
I finger the glass beads I strung and wore
under the pines while the arrests were going on
(transfixed from neck to groin I wanted to save what I could)
They brought trays with little glasses of cold water
into the dark park   a final village gesture
before the villages were gutted.
They were trying to save what they could
—tell me if this is not the same city.

I have forced myself to come back like a daughter
required to put her mother's house in order
whose hands need terrible gloves to handle
the medicinals   the disease packed in those linens
Accomplished criminal I've been but
can I accomplish justice here? Tear the old wedding sheets
into cleaning rags? Faithless daughter
like stone   but with water pleating across
Let water be water let stone be stone
Tell me is this the same city.

This *I*—must she, must she lie scabbed with rust
crammed with memory in a place
of little anecdotes   no one left
to go around gathering the full dissident story?
Rusting her hands and shoulders stone her lips
yet leaching down from her eyesockets tears
—for one self only? each encysts a city.

1997

A LONG CONVERSATION

—warm bloom of blood in the child's arterial tree
could you forget?   do you
remember? not to
know you were cold?   Altercations
from porches   color still high in your cheeks
the leap for the catch
the game getting wilder as the lights come on
catching your death it was said

                              your death of cold
something you couldn't see ahead, you couldn't see

                    (energy: Eternal Delight)

a long conversation

        between persistence and impatience
        between the bench of forced confessions
            hip from groin swiveled
            apart
            young tongues torn in the webbing
            the order of the cities
            founded on disorder

        and intimate resistance
        desire exposed and shameless
        as the flags go by

Sometime looking backward
into this future, straining
neck and eyes I'll meet your shadow
with its enormous eyes
        you who will want to know
        what this was all about

                Maybe this is the beginning of madness
                Maybe it's your conscience . . .

as you, straining neck and eyes
gaze forward into this past:
what did it mean to you?
        —to receive "full human rights"
        or the blue aperture of hope?

Mrs. Bartender, will you tell us dear
who came in when the nights were
cold and drear and who sat where
well helmeted and who
was showing off his greasy hair
Mrs. Bartender tell me quickly
who spoke thickly or not at all
how you decided what you'd abide
what was proud and thus allowed
how you knew what to do
with all the city threw at you
Mrs. Bartender tell me true
we've been keeping an eye on you
and this could be a long conversation
we could have a long accommodation

On the oilcloth of a certain table, in the motel room of a certain time and country, a white plastic saucer of cheese and hard salami, winter radishes, cold cuts, a chunk of bread, a bottle of red wine, another of water proclaimed drinkable. Someone has brought pills for the infection that is ransacking this region. Someone else came to clean birds salvaged from the oil spill. Here we eat, drink from thick tumblers, try to pierce this thicket with mere words.

Like a little cell. Let's not aggrandize ourselves; we are not a little cell, but we are like a little cell.

Music arrives, searching for us. What hope or memory without it. Whatever we may think. After so many words.

A long conversation
            pierced, jammed, scratched out:
                bans, preventive detention, broken mouths
                and on the scarred bench sequestered
                    a human creature with bloody wings
                        its private parts
                        reamed
                            still trying to speak

A hundred and fifty years. In 1848 a pamphlet was published, one of
many but the longest-read. One chapter in the long book of memo-
ries and expectations. A chapter described to us as evil; if not evil,
out-of-date, naïve and mildewed. Even the book they say is out of
print, lacking popular demand.

So we have to find out what in fact that manifesto said. Evil, we can
judge. Mildew doesn't worry us. We don't want to be more naïve or
out-of-date than necessary. Some old books are probably more useful
than others.

   *The bourgeoisie cannot exist without constantly revolutionizing the instru-
ments of production, thereby the relations of production, and with them the
whole relations of society . . . it creates a world after its own image.*

   *In proportion as the bourgeoisie, i.e., capital, is developed, in the same pro-
portion is the proletariat, the modern working class developed—a class of
laborers who live only so long as they find work, and who find work only so
long as their labor increases capital. These laborers, who must sell themselves
piecemeal, are a commodity, like every other article of commerce, and are con-
sequently exposed to all the vicissitudes of competition, to all the fluctuations
of the market.*

58

—Can we say if or how we find this true in our lives today?

She stands before us as if we are a class, in school, but we are long out of school. Still, there's that way she has of holding the book in her hands, as if she knew it contained the answer to her question.

Someone: —Technology's changing the most ordinary forms of human contact—who can't see that, in their own life?

—But technology is nothing but a means.

—Someone, I say, makes a killing off war. You: —I've been telling you, that's the engine driving the free market. Not information, militarization. Arsenals spawning wealth.

Another woman: —But surely then patriarchal nationalism is the key?

He comes in late, as usual he's been listening to sounds outside, the tide scraping the stones, the voices in nearby cottages, the way he used to listen at the beach, as a child. He doesn't speak like a teacher, more like a journalist come back from war to report to us. —It isn't nations anymore, look at the civil wars in all the cities. Is there a proletariat that can act effectively on this collusion, between the state and the armed and murderous splinter groups roaming at large? How could all these private arsenals exist without the export of increasingly sophisticated arms approved by the metropolitan bourgeoisie?

Now someone gets up and leaves, cloud-faced: —I can't stand that kind of language. I still care about poetry.

All kinds of language fly into poetry, like it or not, or even if you're
only
       as we were   trying
           to keep an eye
                on the weapons on the street
                    and under the street

Just here, our friend L.: bony, nerve-driven, closeted, working as a
nurse when he can't get teaching jobs. Jew from a dynasty of con-
verts, philosopher trained as an engineer, he can't fit in where his
brilliant and privileged childhood pointed him. He too is losing
patience: *What is the use of studying philosophy if all that it does for you
is enable you to talk with some plausibility about some abstruse questions of
logic, etc . . . & if it does not improve your thinking about the important ques-
tions of everyday life, if it does not make you more conscientious than any
journalist in the use of the dangerous phrases such people use for their own
ends?*

*You see, I know that it's difficult to think well about "certainty," "probabil-
ity," perception, etc. But it is, if possible, still more difficult to think, or try
to think, really honestly about your life and other people's lives. And think-
ing about these things is NOT THRILLING, but often downright nasty.
And when it's nasty then it's MOST important.*

His high-pitched voice with its darker, hoarser undertone.

At least he didn't walk out, he stayed, long fingers drumming.

So now your paledark face thrown up
into pre-rain silver light your white shirt takes
on the hurl and flutter of the gulls' wings
over your dark leggings their leathery legs
flash past your hurling arm one hand
snatching crusts from the bowl another hand holds close

You, barefoot on that narrow strand
with the iceplant edges and the long spindly pier
you just as the rain starts leaping into the bay
in your cloud of black, bronze and silvering hair

Later by the window on a fast-gathering winter evening
my eyes on the page then catch your face your breasts that light

> *. . . small tradespeople,*
> *shopkeepers, retired tradesmen, handicraftsmen and peasants—*
> *all these sink gradually into the proletariat*

> *partly because their*
> *diminutive capital does not suffice for the scale on which*
> *modern industry is carried on, and is swamped in the*
> *competition with the large capitalists*

> *partly because their specialized*
> *skill is rendered worthless by new methods of production.*

> *Thus, the proletariat is recruited*
> *from all classes of the population. . . .*

pelicans and cormorants stumbling up the bay
the last gash of light abruptly bandaged in darkness

1799, Coleridge to Wordsworth: *I wish*
you would write a poem
addressed to those who, in consequence
of the complete failure of the French Revolution
have thrown up all hopes
of the amelioration of mankind
and are sinking into an almost epicurean
selfishness, disguising the same
under the soft titles of domestic attachment
and contempt for visionary philosophes

A generation later, revolutions scorching Europe:
the visionaries having survived despite
rumors of complete failure

the words have barely begun   to match the desire

when the cold fog blows back in
organized and disordering
muffling words and faces

Your lashes, visionary! screening
in sudden rushes this
shocked, abraded crystal

I can imagine a sentence that might someday end with the word, love. Like the one written by that asthmatic young man, which begins, *At the risk of appearing ridiculous* . . . It would have to contain losses, resiliencies, histories faced; it would have to contain a face—his yours hers mine—by which I could do well, embracing it like water in my hands, because by then we could be sure that "doing well" by one, or some, was immiserating nobody. A true sentence, then, for greeting the newborn. (—Someplace else. In our hopes.)

But where ordinary collective affections carry a price (swamped, or accounted worthless) I'm one of those driven seabirds stamping oil-distempered waters   maimed "by natural causes."

The music's pirated from somewhere else: Catalan songs reaching us after fifty years. Old *nuevos canciones,* after twenty years? In them, something about the sweetness of life, the memory of traditions of mercy, struggles for justice. A long throat, casting memory forward.

"it's the layers of history
we have to choose, along
with our own practice: what must be tried again
over and over and
what must not be repeated
and at what depth   which layer
will we meet others"

           the words barely begin
           to match the desire

and the mouth crammed with dollars doesn't testify

                    . . . the eye has become a human eye
              when its object has become a human, social object

BRECHT BECOMES GERMAN ICON ANEW
FORGIVEN MARXIST IDEAS

. . . the Arts, you know—they're Jews, they're left-wing,
in other words, stay away . . .

So, Bo Kunstelaar, tell us true
how you still do what you do
your old theories forgiven
—the public understands
it was one thing then but now is now
and everyone says your lungs are bad
and your liver very sad
and the force of your imagination
has no present destination
though subversive has a certain charm
and art can really do no harm
but still they say you get up and go
every morning to the studio
Is it still a thrill?
or an act of will?
Mr. Kunstelaar?

—After so long, to be asked an opinion? Most of that time, the opinions unwelcome. But opinion anyway was never art. Along the way I was dropped by some; others could say I had dropped them. I tried to make in my studio what I could not make outside it. Even to have a studio, or a separate room to sleep in, was a point in fact. In case you miss the point: I come from hod-carriers, lint-pickers, people who hauled cables through half-dug tunnels. Their bodies created the possibility of my existence. I come from the kind of family where loss means not just grief but utter ruin—adults and children dispersed into prostitution, orphanages, juvenile prisons, emigration—never to meet again. I wanted to show those lives—designated insignificant—as beauty, as terror. They were significant to me and what they had endured terrified me. I knew such a life could have been my own. I also knew they had saved me from it.

—I tried to show all this and as well to make an art as impersonal as it demanded.

—I have no theories. I don't know what I am being forgiven. I am my art: I make it from my body and the bodies that produced mine. I am still trying to find the pictorial language for this anger and fear rotating on an axle of love. If I still get up and go to the studio—it's there I find the company I need to go on working.

"This is for you
this little song
without much style
because your smile
fell like a red leaf
through my tears
in those fogbound years
when without ado
you gave me a bundle of fuel to burn
when my body was utterly cold
This is for you
who would not applaud
when with a kick to the breast or groin
they dragged us into the van
when flushed faces cheered
at our disgrace
or looked away   this is
for you who stayed
to see us through
delivered our bail and disappeared
This little song
without much style
may it find you
somewhere   well."

In the dark windowglass
a blurred face
—is it still mine?

Who out there hoped to change me—
what out there has tried?

What sways and presses against the pane
what can't I see beyond or through—

charred, crumpled, ever-changing human language
is that still *you*?

1997–98

NOTES ON THE POEMS

CHAR

Page 16: Italicized phrases and some images from *Leaves of Hypnos*, the journal kept in 1942–1943 by the poet René Char while he was a commander in the French Resistance, and from some of Char's poems. I have drawn on both Jackson Mathews's and Cid Corman's translations of Char's journal in integrating his words into my poem. Char joined the Surrealist movement late and broke with it prior to World War II. It was André Breton who said, "The simplest surrealist act consists of going down into the street, revolver in hand, and shooting at random."

MODOTTI

Page 19: Tina Modotti (1896–1942): photographer, political activist, revolutionary. Her most significant artistic work was done in Mexico in the 1920s, including a study of the typewriter belonging to her lover, the Cuban revolutionary Julio Antonio Mella. Framed for his murder by the fascists in 1929, she was expelled from Mexico in 1930. After some years of political activity in Berlin, the Soviet Union, and Spain, she returned incognito to Mexico, where she died in 1942.

In my search for Modotti I had to follow clues she left; I did not want to iconize her but to imagine critically the traps and opportunities of her life and choices.

CAMINO REAL

Page 32: "Can you afford not to make / the magical study / which happiness is?" From Charles Olson, "Variations Done for Gerald Van der Wiele," in *Charles Olson, Selected Poems,* ed. Robert Creeley (Berkeley: University of California Press, 1997), p. 83.

Page 32: "George Oppen to June Degnan: . . ." See George Oppen, *The Selected Letters of George Oppen,* ed. Rachel Blau DuPlessis (Durham, N.C.: Duke University Press, 1990), p. 212.

"THE NIGHT HAS A THOUSAND EYES"

Page 43: The title of the poem is that of a composition played by John Coltrane on the album *Coltrane's Sound*, Atlantic Jazz, 1964.

Page 47, section 5, lines 10–12: *". . . the Lordly Hudson / . . . which has no peer / in Europe or the East."* From Paul Goodman, "The Lordly Hudson," in *The Lordly Hudson* (New York: Macmillan, 1962), p. 7.

Page 48, section 6, lines 9–10: *"—Where do you come from?— / —Como tú, like you, from nothing—."* See Jack Agüeros, Introduction, *Song of the Simple Truth: The Complete Poems of Julia de Burgos,* comp. and trans. Jack Agüeros (Willimantic, Conn.: Curbstone Press, 1997), p. xxv.

Page 50, section 8, line 4: "through *interboro fissures of the mind."* From Hart Crane's "The Bridge," pt. VII: "The Tunnel," line 71.

Page 50, section 8, line 9. In "The Bridge," Crane hallucinated Edgar Allan Poe in the New York subway; I conjure Crane, Miles Davis, Muriel Rukeyser, Julia de Burgos, and Paul Goodman, or their descendants.

A LONG CONVERSATION

Page 53: "energy: Eternal Delight." See William Blake, *The Marriage of Heaven and Hell,* plate 4: "The Voice of the Devil."

Page 55: *"Maybe this is the beginning of madness. . . ."* See Osip Mandelstam, *Selected Poems,* trans. Clarence Brown and W. S. Merwin (New York: Atheneum, 1974), p. 95.

Page 58: *"The bourgeoisie cannot exist . . . its own image."* See Karl Marx, "Manifesto of the Communist Party" (1848), in *The Portable Karl Marx,* ed. Eugene Kamenka (New York: Penguin, 1983), pp. 207–8. *"In proportion as the bourgeoisie, i.e., capital. . . ." Ibid.,* p. 211. See also Karl Marx and Frederick Engels, *The Communist Manifesto: A Modern Edition,* intro. Eric Hobsbawm (London and New York: Verso, 1998).

Page 59: "—It isn't nations any more. . . ." Suggested by Hans Magnus Enzensberger, *Civil Wars: From L.A. to Bosnia* (New York: New Press, 1993).

Page 60: *"What is the use of studying philosophy. . . ."* See Norman Malcolm, *Ludwig Wittgenstein: A Memoir* (London: Oxford University Press, 1958), p. 39.

Page 62: *"small tradespeople . . . of the population."* See Marx, p. 212.

Page 64: *"At the risk of appearing ridiculous."* See Che Guevara, *Che Guevara Reader: Writings on Guerilla Strategy, Politics and Revolution,* ed. David Deutschman (Melbourne and New York: Ocean Press, 1997), p. 211: "At the risk of seeming ridiculous, let me say that the true revolutionary is guided by great feelings of love" ("Socialism and Man in Cuba," 1965).

Page 64: "the memory of traditions of mercy. . . ." See interview with Aijaz Ahmad, in *In Defense of History: Marxism and the Postmodern Agenda*, ed. Ellen Meiksins Wood and John Bellamy Foster (New York: Monthly Review Press, 1997), p. 111: ". . . we certainly need the most rigorous of theories but we also need to have memories of the traditions of mercy and the struggles for justice. It is only there that any true reconciliation of the universal and the particular is really possible."

Page 65: *"the eye has become a human eye. . . ."* Marx, p. 151.

Page 65: *"the Arts, you know. . . ."* Richard M. Nixon, taped in 1972, quoted in Robert Penn Warren, *Democracy and Poetry* (Cambridge, Mass.: Harvard University Press, 1975), p. 36.

Page 68: " 'This is for you. . . .' " After Georges Brassens's "Chanson pour l'Auvergnat," recorded by Juliette Greco on her album *10 Ans de Chansons,* Phillips, 1962.

ACKNOWLEDGMENTS

My thanks to the journals that first published these poems: *Agni:* "Plaza Street and Flatbush"; *American Poetry Review:* "The Art of Translation," "Camino Real," and "The Night Has a Thousand Eyes"; *Long Shot:* "Midnight Salvage" (under the title "From the City of Expectations"); *Luna Review:* "A Long Conversation," "Plaza Street and Flatbush," and "Shattered Head"; *River City:* "For an Anniversary" and "Modotti"; *Sulfur:* "Char," "1941," "Letters to a Young Poet," and "Rusted Legacy"; *The Progressive:* "Seven Skins."

My gratitude to the John D. and Catherine T. MacArthur Foundation for a fellowship 1994–99, and to the Academy of American Poets for the Dorothea Tanning Prize;

—to Al and Barbara Gelpi, for decades of conversation;

—to Hayden Carruth, Jane Cooper, Jack Litewka, Jean Valentine, for enduring and critical comradeship in poetry;

—to Frances Goldin and Steven Barclay, for their integrity;

—and for their words at the edge: to Dionne Brand, Clayton Eshleman, June Jordan, and, especially, Michelle Cliff.

Such thanks are always inadequate.